THE
50 Why's
ABOUT Men

THE 50 Why's ABOUT Men

Understanding Men in Relationships

Dr. Saima Sandhu, LPC, MA, MS, PHD

ARCHWAY
PUBLISHING

Archway Publishing books may be ordered through booksellers or by contacting:

Archway Publishing
1663 Liberty Drive
Bloomington, IN 47403
www.archwaypublishing.com
844-669-3957

ISBN: 978-1-6657-5378-4 (sc)
ISBN: 978-1-6657-5377-7 (e)

Library of Congress Control Number: 2023922861

Print information available on the last page.

Archway Publishing rev. date: 02/19/2024

1 How Do You Know Whether a Guy Is Serious about You or Not?

The idea of finding a man who is serious about you seems almost unreal these days, but there are a few things you can keep in mind if you're trying to figure out if he's worth fighting for. The three most important things to keep in mind are emotional stability, flexibility, and availability. How does he handle your emotions? Does he genuinely care, or does he just brush you off?

Next, how flexible is he about changing plans? Does everything have to be his way, or does he consider what you want as well? Finally, is he available for you when you need him to be or just when he's free and has no plans with anyone else? Basically, his actions will prove if he's serious about you.

Another thing to consider is whether he introduces you to his family and friends. Does he involve you in his life, and does he want to be involved in your life? Does he respect you? The first thing in a relationship is to see whether the person-respects you. If there is no respect, then he will not commit.

In today's day and age, most people communicate through text, so that may be another indicator of his intentions toward you. Are his messages thoughtful, or do they just seem repetitive? If he puts no thought into his primary method of communication, this is a sign that he's brushing you off rather than seeing you as a serious partner.

2

How Do a Guy's Feelings Differ from a Girl's?

Guys are genetically different from girls. While you want them to reciprocate the way you show your feelings, this may not always be the case. The key here is to understand their feelings rather than feel frustrated about a lack of reciprocation. First and foremost, understand their emotional stability. By nature, they are more sexual beings, so to them, sex is the first thing on their minds, while emotions tend to be secondary. This, however, does not mean you will get them to love you by having sex with them. It just means that when they do obtain sex, their interests are usually fulfilled. It seems a little vulgar when we think about it, but the key to a successful relationship is understanding that men are not as emotional as women, so if you want them to reciprocate your emotions 100 percent of the time, you may never feel fulfilled.

For the most part, men are emotionally more stable and don't flip out over emotions as women sometimes do. This may not be pleasing to women in the initial phase of the relationship. However, as life advances, men are more stable in the relationship, and women appreciate this, as it gives a household a stable financial footing, especially with children. Even when men cheat on their partner, the extramarital relationship is often a fling, and as it is seen quite often, the other woman remains the other woman when it comes to divorcing the wife. Men try their best to not end their relationship in divorce.

But when women are involved in an extramarital affair, they often leave their marriage. They are, in general, more inclined toward making decisions based on their emotions, disregarding the instability that this will bring to the current family.

3 Does He Mean the Same Thing You Do When He Says He Loves You?

The first time a girl says, "I love you," her heart is usually racing, and she marks this as a significant moment in the relationship. Therefore, we all want to know what goes through a guy's head when he says the same thing. The spoiler here is that most men usually say it out of obligation—they don't experience the same rush of emotions we do. Most, not all, say it because they feel that's what their partners want to hear. So does that mean men don't experience love? Not at all. Their love has more to do with respect than it does with feelings of butterflies and emotions. They want to give respect while feeling respected too. Real love to them equals commitment, and they commit to women whom they place on a pedestal.

A woman who is genuine, presentable, confident, and spiritually/socially strong is the one many men usually consider committing to. Men don't like women who become doormats—have autonomy and self-respect, and they will respect you, which eventually turns into a stronger bond and love. If he is all these things, he wants a woman who is all of them as well. So he can say he loves you, but you won't know if he means it until he commits.

It is important to be clear on where the relationship stand. By that, I mean if a guy is saying it, does he really mean it? In most situations, as we have discussed above, men mean it; however, there are some men who only use these words to get what they want from a woman—sex. For this reason, knowing if they are being honest is extremely important.

However, there are ways to figure out if he means it when he is saying it. To make sure that you are clear on where your relationship stands, you have to look out for certain nonverbal cues to determine that the person is not playing with you. For instance, sometimes when a guy says,

"I love you," he is not sure whether he is "in love with you" or just has feelings for you. Try to see if he avoids eye contact with you—this could be because he does not want to tell you the truth. You may feel that he is rushing when emotional conversations start, perhaps because he does not want to honestly discuss the truth.

Another sign that he is lying is that he changes stories a lot, like if he gives excuses to avoid some events or to go on trips alone. Going back to the original story and seeing what makes sense would be helpful. Overall, a guy's honesty is reflected in his eyes and in his tone.

Dr. Saima Sandhu, LPC, MA, MS, PHD

4   Do Men Experience Heartbreak as Well?

Yes, they do. However, they tend to overcome it more quickly than girls do. They completely distract themselves if they are heartbroken. After a breakup, we all wonder, *Was it real to him?* You can figure this out by seeing how long it takes him to move on to another relationship. If he moves on in two to three months, he wasn't that heartbroken to begin with. However, some men spend years in pain over the same woman because they keep the memory of her with them forever. Even so, many won't try to get back with you out of self-respect, even if they are heartbroken.

Recovery from a breakup is multifactorial. It depends on the individual's personality, the length of the relationship, the self-esteem of the individual, the type of future relationships, and the reason for the breakup (rejection, cheating, etc.). Recovery from a breakup is a process, and it takes time, especially after a long-term relationship.

There is much research done on this topic, and we have discovered how people in general act when they are going through a heartbreak. Both men and women are affected greatly, and they both experience the pain of a breakup. This is due to many reasons, and the severity of the pain depends on many factors, such as whether the breakup came as a shock and whether the relationship was long term. Some studies have shown that men process breakups differently than women. Men often don't share the pain they feel with others, and they try to cope by distracting themselves. Oftentimes, such distractions happen through new relationships.

Other studies have shown that men have a harder time recovering from heartbreak, and some of them don't ever recover. We also see that if the reason for the breakup was rejection, it often leads to obsession, then denial, which can prevent them from being able to form a new relationship.

Neuroscience shows us that after the breakup, we see a rise in testosterone and a decrease in oxytocin. This shows us that men perhaps go into the dating world and are in a different zone. Since they are not ruminating and analyzing the relationship, it is hard for them to get over it. On the other hand, women use socializing as a coping mechanism, though their self-esteem is usually compromised, and are able to see some positive aspects. The more they discuss, the more they learn where they were at fault. They can perhaps use this to their advantage, learn from their mistakes, resolve those issues, and move on. Men, on the other hand, don't talk about it; it is more likely that they don't take accountability for it and blame their partners. Other coping mechanisms they adopt are usually self-destructive.

Dr. Saima Sandhu, LPC, MA, MS, PHD

5

How Do You Get a Guy to Fall in Love with You?

Here's a question that has no universal answer. We already know that every man is different, but there are a few qualities everyone seeks in a partner. First and foremost, it is important to take care of your appearance and look attractive, as untidiness is a possible turnoff for men. Pick out clothes that flatter your body type, and always be on top of your grooming. This would include making sure your breath smells good, your skin looks healthy, facial hair is removed, and your nails and hair are trimmed. The factors for perceived attractiveness are healthy skin, good teeth, a smiling expression, and good grooming.

Research has shown that men look for physical attractiveness in the initial stages. Once they pass this stage, they move on to the attraction stage, and then they determine whether they have developed feelings for the woman.

The next thing to focus on in the initial days of courtship is balancing the time spent with him. It is important not to be clingy yet give him enough time so you are able to meet his needs. If he feels that your lifestyle is so busy that you are unable to spare time for him, then it will push him away. Understand him and his needs while fulfilling yours as well. Try to understand him first, then expect to be understood. Always maintain your autonomy. Remember you have to be happy within yourself, as no one can make you happy. A guy in your life is not going to bring happiness. Rather, your radiating happiness will attract the guy, and your positive attitude may keep him with you.

Another thing to consider is to look out for his likes and dislikes. For instance, if he hinted that he doesn't like to eat ice cream, it is best to always be mindful of it. For instance, don't offer ice cream and let him know that you remembered that he doesn't like it. When it comes to asking about past relationships, make sure to only discuss this topic if he is comfortable. If he indicates that he is not too keen on discussing it, then don't push him. If he does ask about your past, discuss it only then. However, if you feel that he doesn't want to talk more about it, then look for his comfort level. Don't be someone who lets their emotions get the best of them—it is vital to grasp your emotions and to understand them as well.

Always be mindful when conversing with him. Make him a priority in the conversation—listen, reflect and respond. Show affection with small gestures and, most importantly, be genuine. Remember: don't fall in love; rather, grow in love.

Dr. Saima Sandhu, LPC, MA, MS, PHD

6

What should you do if a guy is "hot and cold"?

Relationships should grow slowly, so it's important not to give him all your emotions at once. You might be tempted to grow emotionally attached to him while he's being nice, but keep your emotions in check while you see how he is for the first few months. Observe his behavior but also keep in mind that he may have other stressors that he may not confide in you about, since you may have not fully developed the relationship where he feels comfortable sharing.

As mentioned before, relationships grow slowly and take nurturing and time. Try to see if this back and forth is consistent. Observe his attitude with other people—is only his behavior with you bothersome, or are there other signs? Communicate how you feel when his behavior is rude and give him time to work on it. This requires patience and emotional control on your end. If you notice his effort then know that the relationship has potential.

7   How do you get a guy to actually listen to what you're saying?

This has more to do about when you should talk to him, rather than what you should say. Choose a good time to talk to him; see when he's in a good mood. This is when you need to pick your battles. Categorize the things you want to communicate to him into three categories: Category A should be the things you can handle, Category B are the things you can deal with but would rather not, and Category C are things you absolutely can't handle.

Once you prioritize what you want from this relationship and have set your boundaries on things you are not able to tolerate, firmly, yet gently communicate this to him but do not be rude to avoid making him feel that he is being attacked. Mention how much this relationship means to you and explain how you want to work on it to make it even better. Observe his response: Is he receptive? If you feel that he is receptive, only then bring up how much it bothers you and how it becomes very difficult for you. You would truly appreciate it if he could work on these issues.

Don't pinpoint every small thing, because chances are that he won't respond well to a thousand demands, but he will respond to a few important ones. It's important to note that listening is a two-way street. He'll listen to you when you listen to him. You can make a guy understand your point quickly, so be thoughtful in what you're going to say. Don't overanalyze it. Talk to him very clearly and don't forget to follow the following method of communication: listen, pause, reflect, and respond.

    Dr. Saima Sandhu, LPC, MA, MS, PHD

8

How do you stop overthinking when in a relationship?

This might have more to do with you than it does with a relationship. If the relationship presents itself with triggers that cause you to be uncomfortable, then chances are that you aren't overthinking; in this case, you simply respond to actions he may be doing. But what do you do if the relationship is fine but you're the one who's simply overthinking?

Here, it is important to distract yourself. The more you delve into your overthinking, the more likely you are to confront him about something that may not even be a problem. As soon as these negative thoughts enter your mind, find an immediate distraction. Remove yourself from situations that trigger you into thinking like this and instead find joy in other things such as family and friends.

Overthinking usually happens when you fail to make the relationship just 10 percent of your life and, instead, let it become all consuming. If you find yourself engaged in negative thoughts and overthinking, tell yourself that you have been wrong before and reframe your thoughts into being more positive. Often, discussing your thoughts with a positive person helps, since they are able to give you another perspective.

9

Should you trust your instincts if you think a guy is cheating on you?

Women often intuitively know when a guy is cheating, but do not mistake this with obsession. If you feel like something is wrong, assess your own thinking first. Why do you feel like something is wrong? Is there reasonable doubt, or could it just be part of your own insecurity? Accusing someone could often lead to unwanted problems, so think carefully before making an accusation. If you feel insecure, bring it up with your partner, rather than accusing them. If their habits suddenly change, think of other reasons why this could have been so before resorting to thinking the worst. If all else fails, have reasonable proof that something is indeed going on.

If you are sure that your partner is cheating, remember that confrontation is not always the solution. If you have invested in the relationship, take charge of your emotions first. When you feel that you are in the right headspace, then decide whether you want to continue this relationship or terminate it. If you decide to continue it, then try to work on the relationship rather than confronting your partner.

It is highly recommended that you work with a therapist to sort out the issues in the relationship. I have seen many couples make stronger bonds and form healthier relationships after an episode of infidelity. It gives both partners a reason to value their relationship more. If confrontation is avoided and love is shown the cheating partner for the most part remains in the relationship. Remember not to define your relationship with infidelity if your partner made a mistake—forgive!

10 Why do men cheat?

Different men have different reasons for cheating. While physical validation may be one and not feeling connected to their partner may be another reason, the most important thing to know is that there is some level of emotional disconnect in the relationship if the relationship faces infidelity. We cannot fathom why men would ruin a good thing that they have by making a mistake as stupid as this one.

The short answer is that some men cheat simply because they want sex elsewhere. They may not be getting enough of it from their partners, or they may be following a self-fulfilling prophecy where they think the more sexual partners they have, the better they are at being a "guy." They may even reason that it's because they didn't want to disappoint their partners with their problems, and one thing then led to another.

While cheating is not black and white, it is hurtful and can take a toll on the relationship—it would require help from a mental health professional to overcome such hurt.

11

If my partner takes too long to reply, should I wait the same amount of time to reply back?

This depends on both of your personalities. For example, if he takes a long time to reply, and you always reply immediately, you may become frustrated quickly. In this scenario, you should wait the same amount of time. Don't constantly look at your phone waiting for the same amount of time to become a reality; instead, distract yourself and set up a schedule for when you'll look at your phone and reply to him. This way, you won't become frustrated when you don't get immediate replies from him.

Additionally, it may not be a sign that anything's wrong if he's sending quality messages when he does reply. However, you can tell if he's just busy or if he's playing games based on when he does reply quickly. If he replies immediately only when he needs something, then it might just be a game to him. Each situation is different, so you need to feel it out. See if it's a habit, and communicate that you would like him to reply more quickly.

Understand that habits take a long time to change. If a person is fixing one habit willingly, it would take approximately ninety days for it to become a habit and then a continuous maintenance phase will go on where relapses are expected. As long as you see him trying, acknowledge his effort and let him know that you appreciate him trying.

12

How do I keep from overthinking if my partner replies late?

The best thing to do when you start overthinking is to stop immediately. This is easier said than done, but when you initially have a negative thought, stop it immediately and think of three positive things. Most of the time, chances are that you are just overthinking, and there is nothing truly wrong. You shouldn't text him repeatedly, because even if you're right about something being wrong, sending more messages will worsen the situation.

If the initial text did cause your partner to suddenly become indifferent, let it go for a day and revisit the situation the next day if he doesn't reply. This will give you a chance to gather your thoughts and allow him to cool off as well. As a result, you will have a better chance at fixing the problem.

Additionally, look at why you're overthinking. Do you have a valid basis for these thoughts? It is vital that you maintain your cool in any stressful situation, not just one involving your partner. This will bring calmness to your personality and will equip you to deal with situations with a more thoughtful approach. Becoming hyperactive and overly emotional is never the solution. You always have a better chance at fixing things if you can keep a check on your emotions.

13   How can I get my partner to communicate more with me?

Communication is the initial sign of interest in a relationship. Therefore, if he doesn't communicate, he might just not be interested. However, if he's just not a talkative person, you may need to understand him rather than blame it on disinterest. Look at the culture he was raised in—this can often be indicative of his ability to communicate often. Perhaps in his family, talking is not a priority, and he may have developed this habit growing up. If this is the case, then nothing may be wrong if he doesn't talk as much.

However, if you want him to be a better communicator overall, then try to understand what he likes to do and do those things so that he is open to listening to your concerns. In every relationship, there needs to be compromise and a give-and-take system—give something before asking in return. Talk to him and communicate how you would like him to respond. Men aren't mind readers, and as much as we idealize the fantasy that they should automatically know everything about us, most times, they don't.

Open and honest exchanges are the basis for healthy relationships, not fairy tales. It may be hard to see a relationship as practical sometimes, but it will definitely help it grow. Romantic notions are sweet, but they may not be ideal in situations where communication is required. Understand that romance is only a small part of the relationship. If a relationship is healthy, romance will follow and become enjoyable; in an unhealthy relationship, romance becomes a burden, and often, a lack of it is blamed for the unhealthy relationship.

Dr. Saima Sandhu, LPC, MA, MS, PHD

14

Do men need to be pushed to commit?

You should never force a man to commit, but it is important that you send him a clear message. Mixed messages never end well—therefore, you should let him know that you either see the relationship working in the long term, and if you don't, you should be clear about that as well. Don't lead him on.

Once you clearly communicate your message, the rest is up to him. Don't remind him every day of commitment or wanting to get married. However, if he is taking too long and doesn't want to commit after a year or so, then you can't force him to do so. This will only end in resentment.

If marriage is your end goal and he doesn't seem to be willing to commit, you should leave him. It may hurt initially, but you will be wasting your time if you're with someone who doesn't value the same goals you do. Instead, focus your energy on yourself and eventually find someone who does want to be with you in the long term.

15

How do you know whether a guy is good for you or not?

When making decisions, we often have three states of mind: the reasonable mind, the emotional mind, and the wise mind. Your decision-making should not include your reasonable mind and your emotional mind. Your reasonable mind will consider what the man in question is offering you, while your emotional mind often just requires the presence of love. Considering only one of these will not allow you to make the right decision because love is not always enough to support a relationship if additional support can't be offered on both sides. Here, you need to create a balance in your thinking to determine whether a guy is good for you or not. Thus, using your wise mind, which is a combination of your reasonable mind and your emotional mind, is best.

Loving someone is not enough to form a healthy and lasting relationship—it is only one part of it. Knowing and analyzing the practical aspects of a relationship is important. Here are some questions you should consider: Are you both compatible, and do you complement each other with your strengths and weaknesses? Do you have a similar outlook on life, and similar goals? Is he fulfilling your emotional and reasonable needs, or do you purely love him for superficial reasons? If the latter is the case, then he might not be the right guy for you.

A combination of love and practical approaches in examining the relationship will give you a balance in the decision- making process—using the wise mind.

16 Should financial stability be an aspect of choosing a good partner?

This may seem a little too practical, not exactly fitting the romantic notion of "falling in love," but it should definitely be an aspect of choosing a good partner. Initially, your emotional mind may be content if the potential partner is not financially stable as your mind is solely using the emotional mind in the infatuation/honeymoon phase. However, to maintain a healthy relationship throughout the years, you want someone who is financially stable. This does not make you superficial, because someone who is financially stable is usually able to bring stability in other forms as well. It shows that he is a good decision maker.

Note: this does not mean he has to be "rich"; rather, choose someone who is responsible. Some points to consider are the following: How does he manage his money? Is he responsible? Does he have the drive to make money? Is he able to hold a job? If he lacks any of these, is he aware that he has problems? Is he willing to work on them?

Even if one partner is making enough to sustain both of them, this may not end up working in the long term because resentment and a lack of respect may come into play. In order for such an arrangement to work, both partners have to be open-minded about one person taking on the responsibility of earning. With mutual agreement and sharing of other responsibilities, a relationship can work.

17   What should you do if a guy doesn't text you back?

Give it twenty-four hours. If he doesn't reply in twenty-four hours, this may be an indication that he simply doesn't want to text you back. When someone is a priority, twenty-four hours is a good amount of time to remember to reply to them. There may, however, be extenuating circumstances—for instance, his phone might have been broken, or he might have lost it. If this happens twice, then it is a sure sign that he just isn't interested in making you a priority.

It may seem easy to say that someone not texting you back is a superficial reason to give up on a relationship, but in today's society, that is the main form of communication. Therefore, if he doesn't reply in twenty-four hours, it shows that he isn't interested in communicating with you. Either way, don't text again, because even if he simply forgot to reply, then he was the one who wasn't interested in making you a priority. Men do remember to reply to people they deem important, so if he doesn't reply to you, you should move on. Even if you really like him, you won't be satisfied in a relationship where you have to constantly push him to remember to make you a priority. A good relationship is one where he remembers to reply to you of his own accord.

     Dr. Saima Sandhu, LPC, MA, MS, PHD

18

How do you know when enough is enough? For example, at what point should you stop letting things go and, instead, simply let him go?

This decision is often the hardest since emotions and rational minds both play strong roles in the decision. There are many reasons to stay in a relationship, even if you feel that you have had enough. Every relationship and every individual is unique. However, in any relationship, it is important to make a list of things that are troubling, as well as the good parts of the relationship. Often, people end up in a loop of negative thoughts and are unable to come out of the loop while they are in the relationship. Once the relationship ends, they start to realize that there were many good aspects to the relationship as well.

It becomes essential to use your wise mind when analyzing your relationship. Think of all the positive aspects: Are they enough for you to hold on to the relationship on that basis? Is there sincerity in the relationship? Are there children involved? Can you work on the relationship and go for therapy?

Infidelity in a relationship often causes irreparable damage. However, if dealt with in a positive way, infidelity can sometimes be a means of building a stronger bond. If the partner is remorseful and willing to work on the relationship, and the other partner values the relationship and is willing to forgive, it is quite likely that the relationship will move up a level in forming a stronger bond. It is important to seek help from a therapist during this process, as healing from a traumatic incident takes time and professional help.

19

What are common red flags to avoid when looking for a potential life partner?

Common red flags are dishonesty and lack of respect. When I say dishonesty, I mean the signs to look out for are whether a person is repeatedly lying to you about things and if they are making excuses. This is a red flag as this clearly shows a lack of respect. Observe the person more to see whether he is genuinely trying or is making up excuses. Is he acknowledging your needs and wants, or is he brushing them off? Don't ignore these signs— try to see if he is trying in any of his actions. If you sense a lack of sincerity, this is a red flag. Honesty and sincerity often reveal how he deals with other people. Is he sympathetic toward other people/situations? How much does he care for his family?

Some other things to look for are the personal characteristics of a person, such as his self-esteem—whether he is bragging or showing off—as this could be a result of his lack of self-esteem or an inferiority complex. If someone is overly declarative of their love initially, this shows that they are not mature enough to understand the intricacies of a relationship as love develops over time. Initially, it is mere attraction, which only turns into love after some time.

If a person is overly critical of others, this is a sign of him holding a negative view of life in general, and this may become a problem in the relationship as you may get a cloudy judgment from him about any situation/people you deal with. A balance is desired between being critical and still holding a positive view of others and situations.

All these issues can be worked on with the help of a therapist. However, if you decide to move on in the relationship with these unresolved issues, there is a good chance that your relationship may be impacted.

Dr. Saima Sandhu, LPC, MA, MS, PHD

20 How can you work toward a healthy relationship?

There are many factors that contribute to forming a healthy relationship. The most essential part is to make sure that the person is genuine. Once this is established, other things can be worked on. Communication is an essential part of a healthy relationship. Learning how to communicate with each other can help in getting a better understanding of each other and help in making other people understand you. Some self-help books can help with learning how to communicate effectively. If possible, try to work with a therapist as learning how to communicate effectively is a process and will take time and practice.

Another key to a healthy relationship is trying to understand the other person's love language. This is important because you may have an idealized notion of how the other person should act, but in most cases, they don't live up to these unrealistic expectations. For example, we may think that a guy should buy flowers and chocolates to show love, and when he doesn't, we'll often become upset. However, it may just be that he shows his love through other methods. He may wait for you every night before going to sleep, or he may clean out your car whenever you need it. If you're able to understand each other's love language, then there's less of a chance that you'll get upset in the long run.

Both partners need to be emotionally intelligent; you need to understand your needs as well as his. To do this, you need to listen to him and avoid arguing all the time. It is important to practice patience and forgiveness. When you feel that you have had enough, which is normal to feel in any relationship, think about all the positive aspects and how much your partner has invested in this relationship.

When you are still not able to let go of the negatives, work on forgiving the person. Practicing patience and learning to forgive is an essential part of forming healthier relationships, as these attributes come from practice and only individuals who have stable personalities are able to practice this in the long run.

Finally, a healthy relationship is one that is respectful.

21

Movies often show fairy-tale relationships. How do real relationships compare to this?

As we all know, reality is often different from the dreams we all have and fairy tales we all have seen. Feeling butterflies has no correlation to reality. Fairy tales often portray the best parts of a relationship because that is what attracts people. No one would watch movies that were completely realistic. In reality, fairy tales represent only a small percentage of a real relationship—specifically, the honeymoon phase.

It's important to distinguish between fairy tales and real relationships because fairy tales usually end when the couple gets together; they never follow through with the rest of their lives. Your relationship can definitely have a few fairy-tale moments, but a healthy relationship cannot be a fairy tale from start to end.

Fairy tales are removed from reality in that they often portray that a person can be rescued and obtain happiness—the phenomenon of Prince Charming coming to rescue his lover, followed by a happily ever after. Yet such a phenomenon is truly far removed from reality. A person has to make himself or herself happy and work on his or her own personal growth to achieve happiness. Your partner can be supportive and can provide you comfort. However, no one can give you happiness.

It is good to watch fairy tales to bring a little romance into your relationship. If you feel that your emotions are aroused from watching them and you are inclined toward feelings outside of your relationship, such as a past relationship, avoid watching them altogether. Try to focus on your current relationship and see how you can improve it with more romance and nurturing. These emotions are short-lived and can create chaos if not controlled.

Be mindful of your emotional needs and your partner's emotional needs. Discuss them with your partner and enjoy your moments together. If you feel that your emotions are overwhelming, contact a mental health professional and seek counseling.

Dr. Saima Sandhu, LPC, MA, MS, PHD

22 My boyfriend doesn't post me on social media. Does this mean he's embarrassed by me or that he simply doesn't want the world to know he's committed?

Most times, he doesn't want the world to know he's committed. Other guys simply want to keep their live private, so they usually don't flaunt their relationship. To know which is the case, see if he keeps other parts of his life private as well. This would indicate that he is prone to the latter.

But if he simply keeps his relationship private, he might not want to show that he's committed. Observe how he treats you around people— does he respect you when he is with friends? Does he introduce you during gatherings? If you feel comfortable with him in all other areas, social media is not something to worry about.

23 Should you panic if a guy is talking to other girls on social media?

This isn't cause for panic right away. Initially, see how he's talking to other girls on social media. While some may find this intrusive, it's acceptable to look through his conversations. Not knowing who he is talking to doesn't benefit your relationship; it just creates doubt in your mind.

When you think about it, people who have been married for years often know who their spouse is talking to. Bearing this in mind, if your goal is to get married eventually, being aware of who the other person is talking to is fine. Don't be argumentative but let him know that you would like to be aware of his conversations to dispel any doubt you may have.

It is important not to obsess over your partner's conversations as a level of trust is crucial in all relationships. Obsessiveness can only make things worse for your relationship as it can hurt you more than help you, and can stimulate an unhealthy curiosity further.

Discussing with your partner how you feel may be a good idea. Try to have the right balance in your thought process and in trusting your partner and communicating this with your partner. If your partner is sincere with you, he will always be sincere about the relationship.

Dr. Saima Sandhu, LPC, MA, MS, PHD

24 How much should you let social media affect your relationship?

The answer to this is zero percent. You shouldn't let social media affect your relationship at all. It is a portrayal of the life others want you to see; not the life they're actually living. Most of the time, what you see isn't the truth. If you see someone posting about their relationship and it looks "better" than yours, take this with a grain of salt.

Everyone has a different love language; focus on yours and your partner's, not someone else's. Furthermore, if you think about social media logically, you know that no one posts a "bad" picture. With this being the case, you are more likely to see the good side of their relationship and not the bad.

Humans are a combination of both their mistakes and successes, but on social media, people often exaggerate the good and minimize or eliminate the bad.

25   Can you "change" a guy?

Many women commit to relationships thinking that they will change all the aspects of the relationship or the people that they are not happy with. Once these are changed, it will be "happily ever after." The reality of this situation is as it sounds—a fairy tale that we all want to come true but never does.

If there is something in a guy that is making you uncomfortable, banish the thought that, once both of you are committed or married, you can change him. In most cases, that thing becomes the source of misery in the relationship. Women start to nag about the habit or whatever makes them uncomfortable; men tend to become stubborn about this very habit; and it becomes a source of conflict leading to many other issues.

What can be done if you are talking to a guy who has some qualities you wish he didn't have? Is it best to end the relationship or continue with the commitment? I suggest that you see what kind of issue it is. Does it have to do with something you'll be able to tolerate for the rest of your life? Are there other qualities that you really appreciate in this person, and can these overcome the dislikes you have for this person?

It is important to use the wise mind in this decision as your emotional mind will tell you to dive in and not worry about the potential hardships, while your rational mind will tell you to focus on all the challenges. Bringing the two minds together and focusing on both aspects is best in deciding whether you want to pursue this relationship further. You know yourself and your situation best. Remember: it is much easier to change yourself than to change others. You should know how much you can change yourself in order to be with this person.

If we assume the "change" in question here is trying to get him to commit, the short answer is that you can't change a guy who doesn't want to commit. Men often know from the beginning if they would like to commit to someone or not. If you "fulfill" his requirements for committing, he will—but this doesn't mean you were able to "change" him or push him into committing. He just found qualities in you that he deemed necessary for commitment.

Do not, however, try to fix or change someone who is "broken." You are in a relationship with him. You are not his therapist. Don't let red flags slide simply because you think you can fix him.

26 How do you create a lasting relationship?

There's no one-size-fits-all solution to this question, but there are a few basic things you can practice to ensure your relationship is in good standing. While we all love the idea of romantic notions, they can't be the basis for sustaining a healthy relationship, which needs to be based on reality, not just fairy tales.

It is important to know how your partner makes you feel but also look for compatibility. Focus on your compatibility and how you complement each other. There are always going to be some differences with any person you get into a relationship with. If you learn to be flexible and learn to communicate effectively, most problems can be resolved in a relationship. Your focus should be on understanding the other person, building a trustworthy relationship, giving respect, and showing affection through small actions.

It is best to ignore the behaviors that you find disturbing and forgive as much as you can. However, ensure that you set your boundaries and never let go of respect. If you respect yourself, others will respect you—and if they respect you, they will want to be with you. Your autonomy and self-respect are important to hold on to.

27

How can you communicate that you would like a man to be more romantic?

Everyone has different personalities, and the truth is that those who are romantic tend to simply have that in their personality. Showing romantic gestures if they are not combined with other requirements of a particular relationship cannot fulfill the needs of the relationship, and the couple stays unhappy. Thus, understand that romance is only a minute part of any relationship, and it can be overlooked if other areas are fulfilled.

On the other hand, men who aren't as inclined to showing romance can't be forced to. Men often see sex as romantic—not giving flowers and chocolates. Instead of trying to force romance, try to understand their love language. They may show their love by taking care of you and being there for you when you need them. They may provide for you even if they don't create a scene straight out of a fairy tale. It is important to note, however, that you shouldn't confuse this with them doing the bare minimum. It may be that they show their love in alternative ways, but this is vastly different from them doing nothing at all.

It is important to consider your relationship as a whole and understand that if it is weak in one aspect, it may be stronger in another aspect.

28

Can you explain how a guy's mind works when they are in a relationship?

During the initial stage of a relationship, most men are not as attached—this is the phase when they are talking to a girl because of the physical attraction. The more one prolongs this stage, the better it is, as during this time, women can get a better understanding of the person without being physically involved. Once this stage is passed, men often get more involved and start contemplating whether this woman is worth committing to.

Your behavior in relationships correlates with your interactions in your childhood. The attachment styles you developed as a child are the basis for how you interact in your relationship as an adult. The three attachment styles are secure attachment, in which one can easily love and be loved by others; anxious attachment style, where people need attention and validation to feel loved; and avoidant attachment style, in which the person needs space in a relationship and complains of feeling suffocated.

Some studies have shown that most men tend to have an avoidant attachment style as they are raised in this way, whereas girls are treated differently in childhood and tend to have a different attachment style. Keeping this in mind, remember to encourage your partner to talk to you, listen to him carefully, and provide encouragement and acknowledgment. This will make him feel safe with you and bring him emotionally closer to you. Often, it is difficult for men to share their feelings as they are not used to feeling vulnerable. If they start to feel secure with you, they will want to be with you.

Dr. Saima Sandhu, LPC, MA, MS, PHD

29 How do you avoid going back to the same guy over and over again?

One of the reasons why you go back to the same person is because you have known him for a long time and he knows your strengths and weaknesses. There is always comfort in talking to people you know inside and out. Once the relationship is over, the conflict is usually out of the picture. When you speak to the person without being in the conflict loop (the loop that becomes hard for most people to escape during the relationship), it gives you a chance to think about the positive aspects of the relationship, leading to you feeling attracted and craving the bond you had formed with them during the relationship. The comfort you get from this is more than the comfort in any other relationship, as your current relationship may have conflicts that you are dealing with and you need a person who understands you and can comfort you with no conflicts involved.

For this reason, it is important to know the reality of the relationship that ended. If there is potential in the relationship, seek help from a therapist to hash out all the issues before you get back together. If there is no potential, it is best to avoid talking to your ex as it will only create problems in your future relationship. Try to work on closure and start working on your personal growth so that you are able to form a lasting relationship with your future partner instead of ruminating on the past.

30   How can you get over a guy?

There are multiple reasons why you may not be able to get over him. For example, if he left you, you may be feeling rejected and only want to get back with him so you can get over these feelings of rejection. Instead of doing this, know that it's okay to feel rejected. Seek help from a therapist to help you get over these feelings rather than staying stuck on him.

Rejection is normal, and with as many people as there are in the world, you need to understand that not everyone will always like you. Another reason you may not be able to get over him is that you have attachment and codependency issues. Identify and address these. You need to understand why you want him so badly. Often, if you're trying to get over a guy, you want it to happen. Chances are that you are having trouble with it not because you're in love with him, but rather because of issues you have with yourself. Once you identify these issues, seek help from others rather than validation from him.

    Dr. Saima Sandhu, LPC, MA, MS, PHD

31

How can you avoid texting a guy that you are trying to get over?

First and foremost, you need to delete everything that reminds you of him. Don't keep his messages where you can see. When you start thinking about messaging him, stop that thought immediately.

Implement a buddy system where you find a friend who will respond to your texts immediately. This way, instead of texting the guy you're trying to get over, you text your friend instead. This can be a good distraction at a time when your emotions are taking over and you are not thinking rationally.

Finally, if he messages you, delete it immediately without reading it. You are more likely to respond to him if you do read it.

32 How much should you "give and take" in a relationship?

All relationships are based on give and take. We have a symbiotic relationship with all human beings, and the moment this balance is disrupted, negative feelings develop. If they are not taken care of, they come to the surface and affect the relationship, eventually leading to many problems.

In my experience with my clients, I have noticed that people are okay with giving as long as they feel that they are being treated fairly. The moment a person feels that he or she is not being treated fairly, resentment develops. Fair treatment in a relationship includes emotional, physical and financial aspects. Try to focus on giving in all these spheres rather than focusing on one. Know your needs and make them known. That way, you don't harbor any feelings of resentment. Balance is key here.

33

How do you get a guy to respect you?

The saying that respect is earned is in fact very true. You have to earn respect in all relationships by making sure your character is strong. Be genuine, honest, hold on to your values and do not deviate from them. If you respect yourself, others will respect you. If you become a doormat and lose respect for yourself, others will disrespect you.

This does not mean that you should not be flexible. It means that you give respect and take respect. Keep your boundaries and make them known in a nice way. Focus on your goals and hold your head up when it comes to good ethical values. Be a positive and giving person. Be the person you want to be known as with him.

Remember that respect isn't freely given—you need to earn it.

34

How far should you go on a first date?

How far you should go on a first date really comes down to your own goals and values. In terms of physical and emotional boundaries, I suggest that you hold back and keep your emotions and physical desires in check. Once you say things, you can never bring those words back, and once you have taken the step to be physically intimate, you can never take that back.

Men have an innate desire to chase a woman until they get their physical desires met. It is best to keep the chase going until you get to know him enough to know if you should really go further with this person.

When you become physically intimate with someone, you make a choice to let them become a part of your life's history that is going to stay with you—the impact that a physical relationship has on a person is far more significant than people actually think. One-night stands have been shown to impact women with low self-esteem, causing feelings of loneliness and being used. Physical intimacy is a means to bring a couple closer and make their love stronger, rather than just an act of lustful desire.

Once a person becomes used to having casual physical intimacy, the brain is trained to keep the two disconnected. However, as we are made to mate with people we love, we should cherish this notion and hold on to being physically intimate with people whom we know we are going to form long-term relationships with. This will only fuel the physical part of the relationship, and what you construe as love will actually be lust. Many women who do this do not end up in lasting and healthy relationships.

The same applies to men. Both partners need to understand that beginning a relationship on a sexual basis often means that it won't last. Men take a while to fall in love, and they never fall in love because of sex.

35

Women often enter relationships with the thought of getting married at the end. Is it the same for men?

There are four stages that a relationship goes through. The first stage is the initial attraction, which entails mostly physical attraction between both individuals. This is usually in the first few meetings, and the relationship moves on to the next stage in which curiosity develops for each other. The physical attraction is still there, along with developing a liking for their other superficial attributes. In this stage, both parties try to impress each other and don't give a thought to the differences between them. During this phase, individuals are not using their rational minds or wise minds; rather, they are using their emotional minds. They are only focusing on emotional satisfaction, rather than considering if the person they are courting is the right person for them. They hardly give a thought to any of the red flags, and if anything becomes apparent, they think they'll be able to change the person in the future.

The next phase is when the couple starts to see their differences and realizes the reality of this relationship. This usually happens within three to four months after the initial contact. In this stage, women are focused on questioning if they should commit to this person or if, in their minds, they have already desired this commitment/marriage. Yet men are not even close to the commitment stage at this time. They are analyzing the relationship and making notes in their brains about how this woman behaves. Is she worth the commitment or not?

If a guy moves on to the next stage, that's when he thinks about commitment/marriage. Thinking about commitment starts in the third phase of the relationship, not in the first or second. If a person jumps into commitment, then that person is not using his or her wise mind as that person is not sure what he or she is getting into. As the old adage goes, "slowly but surely" is the way to go.

36

How should the topic of opposite-sex friends be addressed when you are in a relationship?

This depends on what your values are. If your values are aligned, then it really shouldn't be a problem. However, if they're not, communicate what you can and can't deal with to him. It's completely acceptable to tell him that you don't want him to have female friends. This doesn't come off as controlling or condescending; you are simply relaying your values to him.

If you don't have friends that are men, then he should be okay without female friends as well. You need to be clear with him because letting it build up will cause fights and eventually cause the relationship to disintegrate. Natural comparison starts between girls, and this ruins a relationship. It's fine if he has female coworkers and needs to talk to them, but extraneous friends aren't okay if you have a problem with them. He can find friendship elsewhere if you are that important to him. This is a sacrifice he should be willing to make for your relationship.

37 How can you tell if you're compatible?

Compatibility in a relationship is extremely important as this is the base of your relationship. The first thing to look for is whether both of you have the same values. Sharing the same values will help you navigate life more easily, as both of your perspectives will be similar in situations.

The next thing is to see how you both work through a conflict. All couples have conflicts, and if you are compatible in working through them, then it will make your relationship strong and at ease.

Are you compatible in handling each other's stress? This is extremely important because in life, we do go through many stressful and challenging moments, and if your partner knows how to handle you in these moments, then he can provide you comfort during that time.

Look to see if you support each other's dreams—are you both passionate about each other's dreams? How much effort will you put into supporting each other?

The other compatibility factor to look at is to see if you have the same level of physical intimacy. If you are compatible in physical intimacy, this will help in creating a stronger bond.

If you are compatible in all of the above, you can coexist in this relationship with the least amount of conflicts.

Dr. Saima Sandhu, LPC, MA, MS, PHD

38

Do men become annoyed when you message them constantly?

Yes, they do. As mentioned before, men often tend to be "practical." They may be fine with this initially, but they do end up getting annoyed in the end. In the honeymoon phase of your relationship, they will be amenable to this, but afterward, they will want less of it.

This doesn't mean they're less interested in you. They still want to stay connected without constant messaging. Additionally, they don't enjoy "interrogations." Men who want to control you want to know what you're doing all the time, but they won't want the same thing done to them. Here, they aren't trying to be sweet, but rather trying to establish control.

39 Do men care about a woman's appearance? For example, do they care if she wears makeup or weighs more than the "average" girl?

Physical attraction, no matter how much we deny it, does matter to men. Having said that, it is important to note that who we consider physically attractive varies from person to person. Most men are not looking for extreme levels of beauty—they seek a presentable woman whom they feel attracted to and would be able to present to others. For this reason, it is extremely important to look after yourself and try to keep up with your appearance, even if you hear your partner say otherwise. Keeping up with yourself means that you should look out for clothes that compliment your body shape, put on subtle makeup to make yourself look fresh, take care of your overall hygiene and make sure you use a nice scent daily. If you make this a part of your daily routine, it will become easier to be consistent with this and you won't have to worry about what he is thinking. Keeping up with the things listed above should be done for yourself so you feel good about yourself. Rather than focusing on your flaws or what you lack in looks, focus on how you can make yourself look more attractive as this will give you inner confidence that will radiate from within. Your partner will find you attractive and it will be difficult for him to resist you.

Dr. Saima Sandhu, LPC, MA, MS, PHD

40

How can you tell if a man is just leading you on?

We may think it is really hard to tell if someone is leading you on. By focusing on his behavior, it becomes apparent if he is leading you on. One thing to look out for is if he disappears for periods when he only stays in touch enough to keep you on the hook. A real relationship does require communication—if not multiple times throughout the day, then at a minimum once or twice daily.

If you are in the third stage of a relationship where the attraction part is over, it is time to start observing his behavior and analyze where your relationship stands. He may just be interested in a physical relationship, and the moment you start to ask him for something more, he makes up excuses. He doesn't introduce you to his family/friends. You are on the fringe in his life—waiting to enter at some point. These are clear signs that he is leading you on.

The reason why many women fail to understand these tactics is because men often give them the attention and affection they need in those moments when they desire a physical relationship. As soon as this desire is met, they ghost their partners. Being vigilant for these signs is important and so is keeping your emotions in check at this point, as you may crave those intimate moments and don't want them to end. However, in the long run, you are doing yourself more harm if you stay with him.

So be strong and leave him—work on your personal growth and look for someone who will respect you for who you are, and give you genuine love.

41

How do you keep faith in yourself and the notion that you will find love one day?

You don't need to let the notion of finding love consume you. Remember: this should only be 10 percent of your life. If you work toward your goals and let your life progress, love will find a way to you. Finding love shouldn't be synonymous with deadlines you have set in your life. We can make all the plans we want, but chances are that life will always have other plans in place for us.

Create a balance in your personality and work on yourself—know your flaws and work on personal growth. Measure yourself against yourself as the more you grow personally, the more confident you'll become. This could be from acquiring better communication skills to learning how to be more mindful of your emotions. Reflect on yourself, your desires, your needs, your wants, and your goals. When you become self-aware, the confidence will be apparent in your outward actions, and you will be able to form stronger relationships once the right person comes along.

42   Should you tell men about your past or lie about it?

While you shouldn't blatantly lie about your past, sometimes, full transparency isn't the answer either. Let him know that you would like to keep the past in the past without being completely direct about it. Don't pretend like you're perfect and have never done anything wrong, but just know that sometimes less is more in relationships. Don't bring up the past if you think it will affect your relationship—this is fine as long as you are giving 100 percent to the relationship now. If you don't let your past affect your current relationship, then there is no reason to keep addressing it.

43 How can you handle rejection, as it is very painful?

I t is true that rejection is a very painful experience to go through at any stage in your life. Start by analyzing the situation and be open-minded when you are doing this. When you handle rejection gracefully, you will gain respect for yourself and be able to handle the whole situation in a more positive way. Learn from your rejection and don't let your inner critic take over your emotions.

There are many possible reasons for the rejection—for instance, you may have not been someone's type, or they may have many of their own issues to deal with and may have not been ready to move on in the relationship. If the rejection happened early in the relationship, you saved yourself from a lot of heartache, so always be thankful for this. Don't brush your feelings off; rather, address the pain. Practice mindfulness and stay in tune with your feelings of hurt and address your inner critic.

It is okay to feel hurt as long as you are letting it weigh you down. If you learn to deal with this rejection, know that you'll be going up a ladder in your personal growth as life will always bring some downs. Knowing how to navigate through it gracefully is the key to living a healthier and more fulfilling life.

Dr. Saima Sandhu, LPC, MA, MS, PHD

44

What can you do to keep the guy interested after your initial meetup?

Be genuine—I can't say enough about how being sincere and genuine is important in forming relationships and keeping good people connected to you. Everyone, including you, would want someone who is not going to manipulate them and will care for them.

The next thing to focus on would be paying close attention to him and get to know him from the little details of his life—pay attention to his preferences, dealings, and relationships. Make your initial time all about them by listening to them rather than bringing yourself out. You'll get his attention more if you give him time rather than asking him to pay attention to you. Listen to his stories, his complaints, and his experiences. Remember them. Once he knows that you pay attention to what he is saying and give this importance, he will become closer to you and start sharing more of his vulnerable side. If you succeed in this, you are off to a good start. Keep going, and you will form a healthy relationship.

45

What is the difference between looking for needs and looking for wants when you are looking for a person?

The difference between your wants and your needs is extremely important when you are searching for a partner. Knowing the difference between the two is also very important as your needs are something that you should not compromise on. The needs are values, goals, and ambitions in life. These are considered needs because life's purpose depends on this, and if you don't share this with your partner, you will have a hard time sharing your life with this person.

Wants are intellect, looks, ethnic background, and so on. Often, people focus on the wants more than the needs—one reason for this is that it's easier to find out about the other person's wants before you even start to communicate with them. Even after you start to communicate, many people don't find out about the other person's goals, values, and ambitions as this never comes up in the conversation or people are not clear about these answers themselves.

The first step is to make sure that you are clear about your goals, values, and ambitions in life. Once you know what you want out of life, it will be easier for you to identify people with similar values, goals, and ambitions.

It is important to focus on the needs rather than the wants because you'll notice how wants such as physical attributes and intelligence can change over time. Some of the most intelligent people who didn't keep up with the requirement for keeping up with their optimal brain health lost their intellect, while people who had average intelligence but worked

Dr. Saima Sandhu, LPC, MA, MS, PHD

on their curiosity and did things to optimize their brain health were able to ultimately outperform. The same thing goes with looks—if a person doesn't look after himself and take care of his appearance, he will begin to look sloppy and unkempt.

46   What is a healthy relationship?

Respect, trust, and honesty are the main components of a healthy relationship. Once you have these, you can work on a healthy emotional connection to make your relationship healthy. What I mean by this is that you and your partner make each other feel loved and fulfill each other's emotional needs.

The next thing to focus on is how you disagree with each other. Are you respectful when you are in a conflict? Do you feel safe to disagree or discuss a conflict, or do you feel that you are going to get a retaliation? Are you able to come to terms and resolve your conflicts without humiliating, disrespecting, or degrading the other person? If you are able to do this, then this is a huge success in your relationship as most couples struggle with this. Once you can conquer this step, it is a sign of the growth of your relationship.

The next thing is to maintain autonomy—keep your life outside of your relationship alive. This will boost your mental health and keep your relationship healthy as well. Do things together as a couple and have some of your own interests as well.

Finally, open and honest communication where you are able to make your needs, fears, and desires known is essential. If you are able to build your relationship on this, then you can enjoy the bliss of a healthy relationship. If you are not there yet, you can work your way up as long as you have the main components there to start off a relationship—which are respect, trust, and honesty.

Dr. Saima Sandhu, LPC, MA, MS, PHD

47

When you are in love do you constantly feel that or there are moments when you are not in love?

Love is like any other emotion. Our emotions keep changing, and so does love—it is not static. This does not mean that your base emotions of loving your partner has changed. Rather, it means that the intensity of love that you felt for your partner can change. Thus, constantly nurturing your relationship is important, and this will help in forming bonds that become stronger and are less likely to fade as you get older.

48

If I didn't have a good past (childhood, or good previous relationships), will I not be able to form healthy relationships in the future?

You can always try to grow personally and work on your personal growth. When I say "personal growth," I mean changing your patterns of behavior. When you put in enough effort, you can change your thought process, your feelings, and, thus, your actions. It is helpful to work with a therapist so that you are guided in the right direction for your personal growth and become aware of the behaviors that need to change that would help in forming healthy relationships.

49

If I am not physically attracted to someone, should I still go on getting to know them?

Yes, since initial attraction and forming a lasting healthy relationship are not related. Many people end up with partners whom they were not attracted to initially but, with time, grew to love them and became attracted to them. Remember to always find out if the person you are approaching has the same values, ambitions, and goals in life, as these are essential and will be harder to change.

50 What is meant by nurturing your relationship?

What I mean by nurturing your relationship is to invest in your relationship. You should devote time to your relationship and your partner—spend quality time with all of your attention focused on them. Be open to change in your relationship. Nothing in life is constant, so being flexible will help ease your partner, and it will help you grow as a person and in your relationship.

Try to bring humor to your relationship, as constantly talking about serious issues can make things very stressful. Smiling and laughing at small things can help with small aggravating situations. However, remember not to use humor to hide your aggravating emotions as it can backfire on you. Be sure you are both on the same page before you make a joke.

Dr. Saima Sandhu, LPC, MA, MS, PHD

www.ingramcontent.com/pod-product-compliance
Lightning Source LLC
Chambersburg PA
CBHW061048120326
41111CB00008B/426